The Peekapak Pals and the New Student

Peekapak

Peekapak

The Peekapak Pals and the New Student
1st Peekapak Publishing ed.
Version: PK

Summary:

ISBN 13: 978-1-988879-06-2
ISBN 10: 1-988879-06-X

Meet the Class!

Menka
loves building
things using blocks.

Leo the Hedgehog
really likes learning
how things work.

Cody
loves drawing
pictures —especially
comic books!

Saffron the Skunk
is great at cooking
and making new
recipes.

Lucia
uses electricity
to make everything
light up!

**Sebastian the
Salamander**
loves new
technology.

The Peekapak Pals live in Peekaville, a colorful town filled with many adventures!

Kenji
designs amazing clothes.

Brady the Bunting
dances to music he creates.

Inés
loves computers and building apps.

Freya the Fox
takes lots of pictures and videos.

Apollo
loves robots and always wants to build new ones.

Zoey
is really into helping plants grow.

There's a new student in class!
Her name is Inés.

Cody tries talking to Inés.

But she doesn't want to talk.

The class tries talking to Inés together.

They tell Inés how great Peekaville is.

But Inés doesn't want to hear about Peekaville.

The class leaves Inés alone.

Leo the Hedgehog wonders if Inés feels nervous and alone, like he did on his first day of school!

Leo sees Inés at the library with a book written in a different language.

Leo asks Inés if he may sit with her.
To his surprise, she nods.

After a few minutes, Leo asks Inés about her book. She says it's about the town where she used to live.

Inés says she misses her hometown very much.

Inés's eyes fill with tears. She talks about her friends and family and how sad she feels about moving away from them.

Leo listens.

Leo tells Inés he's glad she told him how she feels.

Inés thanks Leo for listening.

Leo invites Inés to join him and some friends at the ice cream parlor.

PEEKAVILLE PUBLIC LIBRARY

Everyone is so happy to see Inés.

Inés and Cody have the same favorite dessert: a banana-berry sundae with French fries on top!

After, the friends play berryball.

Inés loves berryball! In her hometown, she calls it *balonbaya*.

Inés starts to think that maybe Peekaville isn't so bad after all!

www.ingramcontent.com/pod-product-compliance
Lightning Source LLC
Chambersburg PA
CBHW042122040426
42449CB00003B/144